Walt Disney PICTURES'

OLIVER & Company

Movie Storybook

By Justine Korman
Illustrated by Al White Studios
Willy Ito
Ron Dias

A GOLDEN BOOK • NEW YORK
Western Publishing Company, Inc., Racine, Wisconsin 53404

 Library of Congress Catalog Card Number: 88-80714 ISBN: 0-307-11995-5/ ISBN: 0-307-61995-8 (lib. bdg.)
A B C D E F G H I J K L M

The sign on the box on the pavement read, "Kitties Need Home." Inside the box was a crowd of playful kittens, all trying to attract the attention of the people passing by. The ginger-coloured kitten jumped and meowed, but he kept getting pushed to the back of the box. Somehow the hands that gently reached into the box never reached for him. Finally the kitten was alone. He was hungry, so he decided to jump out of the box and see what he could find on the city streets.

Soon he met a streetwise dog named Dodger, who said he knew how to get some of the street vendor's delicious sausages. Dodger chased the kitten up the man's shirt, and while the man struggled with the clawing kitten, Dodger grabbed the sausages.

"Let's eat!" the kitten exclaimed, already tasting his long-overdue breakfast.

But Dodger laughed and said, "See ya 'round, kid."

"That's not fair!" the kitten protested.

"Fairs are for tourists," Dodger called over his shoulder. And he ran away with the sausages.

Dodger arrived at his gang's headquarters, a barge owned by a man named Fagin. The rest of the gang was inside, arguing over who was supposed to have brought home food for their supper.

"It was your turn, Frankie," whined Tito, the Chihuahua.

"My name is Francis, not Frankie," the bulldog replied in lofty tones.

"Man, your name will be mud when Fagin gets here and there's nothing—" Tito stopped in mid-sentence as a chain of sausages landed at his feet.

"New York's coolest canine comes through again," Dodger declared, stepping into the light. "But not without a struggle."

Dodger went on to brag about the terrible monster he fought off to get the sausages.

"He had sharp fangs and razor-sharp claws... Look out! The roof!" Dodger yelled, running for cover as part of the roof of the barge caved in.

Tito tiptoed timidly toward the wreckage. He sniffed, and a claw raked across his nose.

"Hey! It's an alien!" Tito shrieked.

"What's an alien?" wondered big, dumb, but lovable Einstein.

"Cool it, guys. It's just a cat," Dodger said.

When the little cat explained that he'd followed Dodger because he wouldn't share the sausages, the rest of the gang had a good laugh. "You're awfully cute for a monster," Rita teased, patting the kitten's soft coat.

"Shh!" Dodger hissed. They all listened for a moment, until Dodger said, "It's Fagin."

The dogs greeted Fagin with licks and wagging tails. To most people Fagin did not seem important, but to the dogs he was king. The gang proudly displayed the loot they had collected for him, but Fagin was disappointed. Fagin picked up the box and looked inside it.

"A broken tennis racket, an empty wallet, and...a cat?!"

A car horn sounded outside, and Fagin jumped.

"Yikes, it's Sykes!" Fagin exclaimed.

Sykes was an evil man to whom Fagin owed money. And Sykes could be awfully mean about getting his money back.

While Fagin begged for more time to pay, Sykes's Dobermans, Roscoe and DeSoto, boarded the barge. Roscoe hurled insults at various gang members. DeSoto just followed his nose. Then he chuckled, displaying a row of sharp teeth.

The kitten pushed farther into his hiding place between a box and a pail. But there was no fooling DeSoto's nose.

"I like cats," DeSoto growled, catching sight of the kitten. "I like them for supper!"

Just as DeSoto was about to bite, the kitten scratched his nose. The dog fell back yelping, and the barge erupted in a mad chase. The furious Dobermans soon had the kitten cornered. He closed his eyes and awaited the worst. But Dodger leapt between the dogs and the cat.

"If you insist on being the main course, Dodger..." Roscoe growled.

"We'll have your kitty for dessert," DeSoto added.

But Sykes's car horn blared angrily outside. Sykes did not like to be kept waiting. As the Dobermans trotted away Roscoe called, "We'll get you next time, Dodger, and your little cat, too!"

Fagin and his gang were so impressed with the kitten's bravery that they made him a member of the gang. That night, after Fagin read a bedtime story, the kitten curled up next to Dodger.

"This is almost a home," the kitten thought, glancing around at the gang members all cosy in the barge. But when he fell asleep, the little ginger-coloured cat dreamed of a real home with someone who loved him.

The next day the gang hit the streets early, determined to bring home lots of money to save Fagin from Sykes.

"All right, the chauffeur shuffle!" Tito exclaimed as a long black limousine glided into view and stopped nearby.

While Einstein and Francis distracted the chauffeur, Tito and the kitten crept into the car. Tito began busily working on the radio wires. The kitten heard a noise from the backseat and jumped. His paw hit the ignition key and set off a noisy alarm. The gang fled, but the kitten was caught in the wires. He tugged and tugged, but he was trapped and helpless. Suddenly the glass partition slid open to reveal a passenger in the backseat.

The passenger was a sweet little girl who smiled at the kitten and gently helped to free him.

"You poor little thing," the girl cooed. "You look like you need a home. Winston, please take me home so we can give this kitty something to eat."

To Dodger's dismay, the car drove away with his kitten friend inside.

The kitten soon found himself in a beautiful home with a bowl of cream in front of him. He pinched himself, but he wasn't dreaming. The bowl of cream was not only real, it was sweet and delicious.

But it wasn't just the food or the luxurious town house that gave the kitten a warm, happy feeling. He already knew that the little girl, Jenny, was the special someone he had dreamed about.

"I never want to lose you," Jenny told the kitten. She gave him a name—Oliver—a collar, and an identification tag. Then she hugged him, and Oliver purred contentedly.

The only one who wasn't happy about Oliver was the family's pampered poodle, Georgette. "I can't share my home with that cat. What will they say at the Kennel Club?" fretted Georgette. She sat down in front of her heart-shaped mirror.

Georgette shrieked when she saw that her reflection wasn't the only one in the mirror. A gang of street dogs had somehow broken into her house.

"Shh! We've only come for our cat," Dodger whispered. "We're his friends and we want to take him home."

Georgette was more than happy to help.

She showed Dodger and the gang to Jenny's room, where Oliver was curled up asleep on the bed. Then she pinched him, without anyone seeing, so the kitten woke up with a cry.

"See? He's terribly unhappy here. You must take him back with you right away," Georgette said.

And before Oliver could meow a word, he was stuffed into a pillowcase and carried down the fire escape, back to Fagin's barge. While the gang congratulated themselves on the successful rescue, Oliver explained about having a real home with Jenny.

"Why, you ungrateful...cat!" Dodger growled. "Go on back to Fifth Avenue, if we're not good enough for you."

"Fifth Avenue?" Fagin muttered. Seeing Oliver's I.D. tag gave him an idea. He sent a note to the town house, saying he'd found Oliver and wanted a reward for his return.

Soon Jenny and Georgette arrived. Jenny offered Fagin her piggy bank in exchange for Oliver. Fagin was surprised. He had expected a rich grown-up to come for Oliver, not a sweet little girl. He felt so ashamed that he gave Oliver back to Jenny for free.

But then Sykes drove up, demanding payment—from Fagin or anyone else. When Fagin told Sykes he didn't have his money, Sykes became angry. Then he had an idea. Sykes grabbed Jenny and pulled her into the limousine. "I'm sure someone will pay a nice ransom for a little rich girl like you," Sykes said as the limousine sped down the street.

Fagin and his gang were determined to help Oliver and Georgette get Jenny back. They jumped onto Fagin's broken-down motor scooter and followed the limo to Sykes's warehouse.

"Man, this isn't going to be easy," Tito fretted, seeing the warehouse's locked metal doors.

"There's more than one way to skin a cat—sorry, Oliver," Dodger said. "I've got a plan."

Soon Oliver was sitting on one end of a seesaw, inside a football helmet, while Francis balanced on a nearby stack of crates.

Francis jumped onto the other end of the seesaw, and Oliver went flying through the air. He crashed through the warehouse window and landed, safe and sound inside the helmet, on a pile of shattered glass.

Oliver unlocked the door for Georgette and the gang. They tiptoed through the warehouse to Sykes's office, where Jenny was tied to a chair.

Tito and Francis made a lot of noise to lure Sykes away from Jenny. The moment Sykes stepped out of his office the others slipped in and untied the little girl.

"We did it!" Georgette squealed excitedly.

But when Einstein heaved open the heavy sliding door of the warehouse, Sykes and the Dobermans were on the other side.

"Well . . . this has all been very entertaining," Sykes hissed. "But the party is over!"

Just then Fagin crashed through a window on his three-wheeled motor scooter and landed right between Sykes and the gang.

"Get on!" Fagin urged, gunning the motor.

Paws flailing and tails wagging, Oliver, Georgette, and the gang charged past the astonished Sykes and his dogs and jumped onto the scooter—*with* Jenny! But the villains wasted no time jumping into their limo. The chase was on!

Sykes was gaining on them. Down the dark street Fagin saw the subway entrance. He gripped the handlebars tight and steered straight down the stairs.

"Safe at last," Fagin thought. Then he stared back in amazement at the blinding glare of headlights as the limo bounced down the steep steps.

"Hold on to your seats!" Fagin yelled, and he drove the scooter over the edge of the platform and onto the train tracks.

And still Sykes followed!

The limo lurched forward and bumped the scooter. Jenny fell back onto the car's bonnet. Sykes grabbed Jenny's arm, and she screamed.

Oliver leapt onto the limo and bit Sykes's hand until he let Jenny go. Sykes shook the crazed cat onto the backseat, where the Dobermans savoured their moment of triumph.

"You scratched the wrong nose, kitty," snarled DeSoto.

But before DeSoto could bite, Dodger dived through the sunroof and into the fight.

"There's a train coming!" shrieked Georgette. The warning gave Fagin just enough time to steer onto the other track.

But the limo was totally wrecked.

"Oh, no! Poor Oliver!" Jenny cried.

Just then Dodger coolly stepped out of the shadows. He held the motionless kitten by the scruff of his neck.

"Oliver! Oliver, please be all right!" Jenny sobbed as she gently stroked the kitten's fur.

"Mee...meow," Oliver said weakly. His eyes opened, and when he saw Jenny he purred happily.

Oliver purred all through Jenny's birthday party, which was the very next day. She held a grand feast at the town house for all their friends. There was cake, ice cream, bones, and dog biscuits. Everyone was in the happiest mood.

"You can make a wish, too," Jenny urged Oliver as she took a deep breath to blow out the candles.

But Oliver's wish had already come true. He had found the home of his dreams.

NO LINE ON THE HORIZON

U2

WISE PUBLICATIONS
part of The Music Sales Group
LONDON / NEW YORK / PARIS / SYDNEY / COPENHAGEN / BERLIN / MADRID / TOKYO

Exclusive distributors:
Music Sales Limited, 14-15 Berners Street, London W1T 3LJ, UK.
Music Sales Pty Limited, 20 Resolution Drive, Caringbah, NSW 2229, Australia.
Order No. AM997238 ISBN: 978-1-84938-065-2

Music arranged by Derek Jones.
Project Editor: Jenni Wheeler.
Music engraved by Paul Ewers Music Design. Book design by Four5One°Creative, Dublin.
Photography by Anton Corbijn.
Printed in the EU.

NO LINE ON THE HORIZON

Words by Bono
Music by U2, Brian Eno & Daniel Lanois

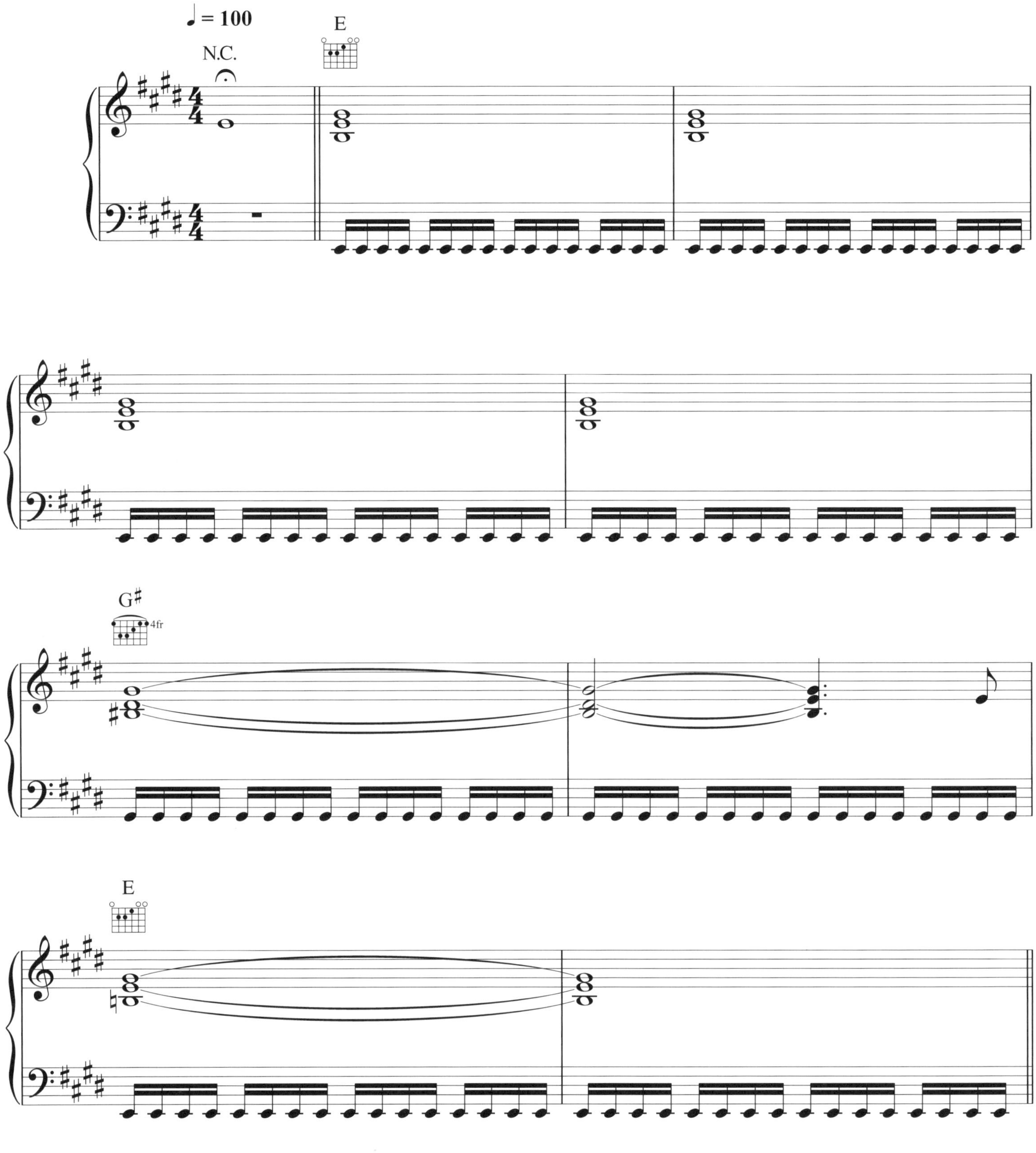

E
1. I know a girl_ who's like a sea.
2. I know a girl,_ a hole in her heart,
I watch her chang - ing ev - 'ry day for me. Oh,_
she said in - fin - i - ty's a great place to start._
G♯
4fr
_ yeah. Oh,_
Oh,_
E
oh._
oh._

E
One day she's still, the next she swells.
Time is ir - rel - e - vant, it's not li - ne - ar.
You can hear the u - ni - verse in her sea shells. Oh,
Then she put her tongue in my ear. Oh.
G♯
4fr
yeah.
Oh,
Oh,
oh.
oh.

C
Am
No, no line on the ho - ri - - i - zon.
E
No, no line.
C
Am
No, no line on the ho - ri - - i - zon.
E
To Coda
No, no line.

E
Oh.
A
Oh, oh. Oh, oh.
E
Oh.
A
Oh, oh. Oh, oh. The

F♯m
songs in your head are now on my mind. You
B7
put me on pause and tried to re - wind.
G
D
C♯
Your love and re - play.
B

E
Ev - er - y night I have the same dream.
I'm hatch - ing some plot, schem - ing some scheme oh,
G♯
4fr
yeah. Oh,
E
oh.

E
I'm a traf - fic cop, rue de Ma - rais.
The si - ren's wail - ing but it's me that want's to get a -
G♯
4fr
- way. Oh,
E
oh.
D.S. al Coda

Coda
E
G♯
4fr
E
N.C.
8va

MAGNIFICENT

Words by Bono & The Edge
Music by U2, Brian Eno & Daniel Lanois

Original key F♯ minor

Gm
Dm
B♭
F
Mag -
C
Cm
Gm
- ni - fi - cent.
Dm
B♭
F
C
Oh, oh. Mag - ni - fi - cent.
N.C.

Gm
Dm
B♭
1. I was born, I was
2. I was born, I was
F
C
Cm
born to be with_ you__ in this space and
born to sing for__ you.__ I did-n't have a
Gm
Dm
B♭
time. Af - ter that and ev - er
choice to lift you up and sing what-
F
C
Cm
af - ter I have-n't had a clue. On - ly to break
-ev - er song you want - ed me to. I give you back my

Gm
3fr
Dm
B♭
rhyme, this fool - ish - ness can leave a
voice from the womb. My first
F
C
Cm
3fr
heart black and blue.
cry, it was a joy - ful noise.
Oh, oh.
Oh, oh.
Gm
3fr
Dm
B♭
F
On - ly love, on - ly love can

C
Cm
3fr
Gm
3fr
leave such a mark.
But on - ly
Dm
B♭
F
love,
on - ly love can
1.
2.
C
Cm
3fr
Cm
3fr
heal such a scar.
(𝄋) u - nite our hearts.
Gm
3fr
Dm
B♭
Just - i - fied till we die, you and I will mag - ni - fy.

F
To Coda
C
E♭
6fr
Oh, oh. Mag - ni - fi - cent. Mag -
B♭
Dm
G
- ni - fi - cent. Oh, oh. Ooh.
G5
3fr
Ooh.

Gm
3fr
Dm
B♭
Vocal ad lib.
3
3
1.
2.
F
C
Cm
3fr
D.S. al Coda
Coda
C
Cm
3fr
C
-ni - fi - cent.
Mag - ni - fi - cent.
Cm
3fr
C
Cm
3fr
N.C.
Mag - ni - fi - cent.

MOMENT OF SURRENDER

Words by Bono
Music by U2, Brian Eno & Daniel Lanois

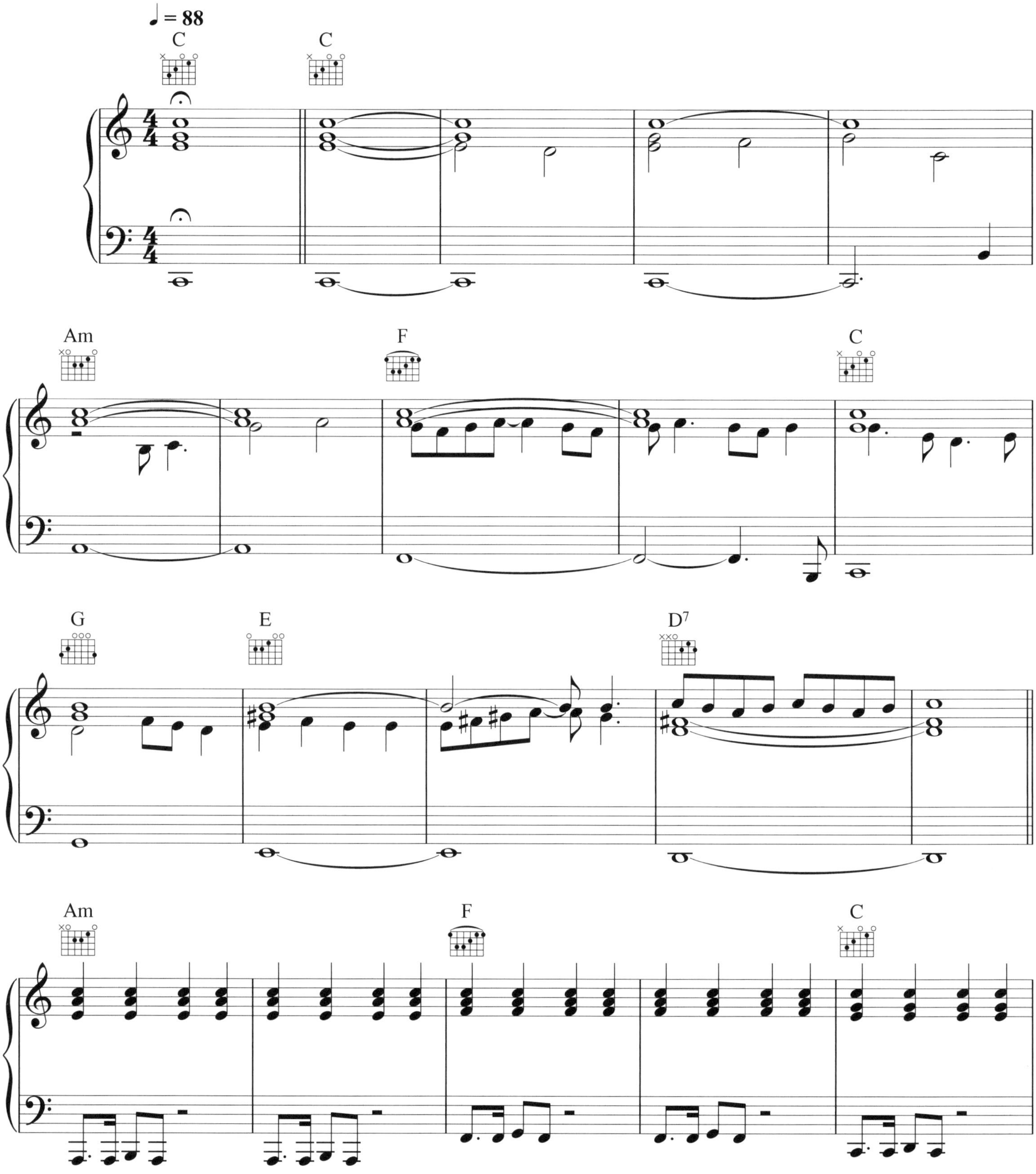

G
E7
D
Am
F
1. I tied my-self with wire to
C
G
let the hors-es run free.
I'm play-ing with the fire till the
E
E7
D
fire play with me.
Mm.

Am
F
2. The stone was sem - i - pre - cious, and we were bare - ly con - scious.
3. We set our - selves on fire, oh girl, could not de - ny her.
C
G
E
Two souls too smart to be in the realm of cer - tain - ty, e -
It's not if I be - lieve in love if love be - lieves in me.
1.
2.
D
D/C
- - ven on our wed - ding day. At the
Oh, be - lieve in me.
F/C
C
mo - ment of sur - ren - der I'm fall - ing to my knees.
3

C
Am
G
I did not no-tice the pass - ers - by and they
F
Am
did not no-tice me.
4. I've
F
been in ev-'ry black hole at the al-tar of a dark star.
C
G
E7
My bod-y's now a beg-ging bowl, it's beg-ging to get back,

D
beg - ging to get back to my heart and to the rhy - thm of my
Am
Fm
soul. And to the rhy - thm of my con - scious - ness.
C
To the rhy - thm that yearns
G
E7
to be re - leased from con - trol. 1. I was

F/C
C
F/C
punch - ing in the num - bers at the A. T. M. ma - chine
2, 4. mo - ment of sur - ren - der of vi - sion o - ver vis - i - bil - i -
3. speed - ing on the sub - way through the sta - tions of the cross.
C
Am
G
I could see in the re - flec - tion a face
- ty I did not no - tice the pass - ers - by and they
Ev - 'ry eye look - ing ev - 'ry o - ther way count - ing
1, 3.
2, 4.
F
F
To Coda
star - ing back at me. 2. At the 4° Oh, oh.
did not no - tice me. 4. At the
down till the pain would stop.

Am
F
Instrumental
C
G
E7
D
1.
Repeat ad lib.
2.
D.S. al Coda
3. I was
Coda
Am
F
oh.
Oh, oh, oh.

C
G
E7
Oh, oh, oh, oh, oh.
1.
D
Oh, oh, oh.
Oh, oh.
2.
D7
D5
5fr
Am

UNKNOWN CALLER

Words by Bono
Music by U2, Brian Eno & Daniel Lanois

5.
Sun - shine. Sun - shine.
Sun - shine. Sun - shine.
G
C/G
G7
Dm
Oh.
Am
C
G
Oh.

C/G
G7
Dm
Oh.
Am
C
Oh.
1. I was
Am
C/G
Fmaj7
lost between the mid-night and the dawn - ing,
(2.) right there at the top of the bur - den.
3
Em
Am
C/G
in a place of no con - se - quence or com - pa - ny.
On the edge of the known u - ni - verse where I want-ed to
3

F
Am
Three thir - ty three when the num -
be. I had driv - en
C/G
F
Em
-bers fell off the clock face. Speed
to the scene of the ac - ci - dent. And I
Am
C/G
F
dial - ling with no sig - nal at all.
sat there wait - ing for me.
G
Em7
Go, shout it out
Re - start and re-boot your - self,

G7
Dm
Am
and rise up. Oh.
you're free to go. Oh.
Oh.
Oh.
C
G
Es-cape your-self and grav-i-ty. Hear me, cease to speak
Shout for joy if you get the chance. Pass-word, you
Em7
G7
Dm
that I may speak. Shush now. Oh.
en-ter here right now. Oh.
Am
C
1.
Oh.
Oh.
Force quit and move to trash. 2. I was
You know your name

2.
G
Em7
G7
so punch it in. Hear me, cease to speak that I may speak. Shush now.
Dm
Am
C
Oh.
Oh.
Don't move
Am
or say a thing.
G
C/G
G7

Dm
Am
C
G
C/G
1-3.
4.
G7
Repeat ad lib.
G
C/G
G
C/G
G
C/G
G

I'LL GO CRAZY IF I DON'T GO CRAZY TONIGHT

Words by Bono
Music by U2

Csus4
C
E/G♯
Knows I'll go cra - zy if I don't go cra - zy to - night. There's a part of me in the
Am
D/F♯
G
cha - os that's qui - et. And there's a part of you that wants me to ri - ot.
Csus4
C
2. Ev - 'ry - bod - y needs to cry or needs to spit.
(3.) Pit - y the na - tion that won't lis - ten to you boys and girls
Csus4
C
Ev - 'ry sweet tooth needs just a lit - tle hit.
'cause the sweet - est mel - o - dy is the one we have - n't heard.

E/G♯
Am
Ev - 'ry beau - ty needs to go out with an id - i - ot.
Is it true that per - fect love drives out all fear?
D/F♯
G
E/G♯
How can you stand next to the truth and not see it? Oh, a change
The right to be ri - di - cu - lous is some-thing I hold dear. Oh, but a change
Am
Em
of heart comes slow.
of heart comes slow.
It's not a
C
Am
G
F
C/E
F
hill it's a moun - tain as you start out the climb.
Do you be - lieve
2° Lis - ten for

C
Am
G
Dm
me or are you doubt - ing?
Oh, we're gon - na make it all the
me I've been shout - ing
𝄋 Let's shout in - to the dark - ness, squeeze
F
Dsus4
Fadd9
To Coda ⊕
way to the light. But I know I'll go cra - zy if I don't go cra - zy to - night.
out sparks of light. You know me
1.
C
Csus4
C
3. Ev - 'ry gen - er - a - tion gets a chance to change the world.

2.
C
G D Am G D
Ba - by, ba - by, ba - by, I know I'm not a - lone.
C G D Am
Ba - by, ba - by, ba - by, I know I'm not a -
G D C C Am
- lone. Ha, ha, ha!

G
F
C/E
F
C
Am
Oh.
D.S. al Coda
F
Gsus4
G
Oh.
Oh, it's not a
Coda
Dm
F
gon - na go cra - zy. You know we'll go cra - zy. You

Dm
F
know we'll go cra - zy if we don't go cra - zy to - night.
C
Oh.
Slow - ly now.
Oh.
On - ly slow.

STAND UP COMEDY

Words by Bono
Music by U2

D
A/C♯
A
B
stand up, the wire_ is stretched in be - tween_ our two tow - ers.
can I stand up to beau - ty. Dic - ta - tor of the heart. I can
small child cross - ing an eight lane high - way on a voy - age of dis - cov - er - y.
F♯7(OMIT3)
Stand up in the diz - zy world_ where a love - sick eye can steal_ the view. Not gon - na
stand up for hope, faith, love but while I'm_ get - ting ov - er cer - tain - ty.
Stand up to rock stars. Na - po - le - on is in_ high heels.
D
A/C♯
A
B
fall down_ if I can stand up_ for your love._
Stop help - ing God a - cross the road like a lit - tle old la - dy.
Jo - se - phine be care - ful of small men with big i - deas.

1.
N.C.
2, 3.
A
B
C♯m
A
Ooh,
ooh.
Ooh,
B
C♯m
A
B
C♯m
ooh.
Out from un-der your beds.
B
B♭
A
G♯
To Coda
Come on you peo - ple, stand up for your love.

N.C.
D.S. al Coda
3. I got - ta
Coda
N.C.
Mm.
Mm.
Mm.

B
Em/G
Asus2
B
Em/G
Asus2
B
A
God is love. And
G♯m
4fr
G
love is e - vo - lu - tion's ver - y best
N.C.
day. (sound effect)

A B C♯m A
4fr
Soul rock - in' peo - ple mov - in' on. Soul rock - in' peo-
B C♯m B B♭ A G♯
4fr 4fr
- ple on and on. Come on you peo - ple, we'll move the stars.
B B♭ A N.C. N.C.
Come on you peo - ple, stand up then sit down for your love.
Vocal ad lib.

GET ON YOUR BOOTS

Words by Bono
Music by U2

you see it too? Night is fall-ing ev-'ry-where, rock-ets at the fun-fair.
ghosts aren't real. Here's where we got-ta be, love and com-mu-ni-ty.
1.
Sa-tan loves a bomb-scare, but he won't scare you.
Laugh-ter is e-ter-ni-ty if joy is real.
Hey! Sex-y boots. Get on your
2.
G5
3fr
boots, yeah. 2.You You

A♭5 G5 A♭5 G5
4fr 3fr 4fr 3fr
don't know how beau - ti - ful. You
B♭5 E♭5 F5 G5
6fr 6fr 3fr
don't know how beau - ti - ful you are. No
(Vocal ad lib.)
A♭5 G5 A♭5
4fr 3fr 4fr
you don't know how beau - ti - ful you
G5 B♭5 E♭5
3fr 6fr 6fr
are. You don't know how beau - ti -

F5
To Coda
N.C.
ful you are.
3. That's
N.C.
some-one's stuff they're blow-ing up, but we're in-to grow-ing up, wom-en of the fu-ture hold the
big re-ve-la-tions. I got a sub-ma-rine, you got ga-so-line.

I don't wan-na talk a-bout wars be-tween na - tions.
Not right
now.
Sex - y boots.
Get on your
D.S. al Coda
boots, yeah.
Boss-y boots.
Coda
N.C.
are.
Sex-y

boots. Vocal ad lib.
Sex-y boots.
N.C.
Let me in the sound. Let me in the sound. Let me in the sound sound. Let me in the
Drums
sound sound. Let me in the sound.
cont. sim.
Let me in the sound. Let me
in the sound now. God, I'm go-ing down. I don't wan-na drown now. Meet me in the

sound.
Let me in the sound. Let me in the sound. Let me in the
sound sound. Let me in the sound sound. Meet me in the sound.
N.C.
Get on your boots.
Play 5 times ad lib.
Get on your boots.
Hey, hey, hey!
5
5
5
5

FEZ – Being Born

Words by Bono
Music by U2, Brian Eno & Daniel Lanois

E♭
6fr
+ 8va
Ooh.
B
Ooh.
Ooh.
F♯
Ooh.
Ooh.
C♯
4fr
N.C.

♩ = 94
Dm
B♭6
Csus2
B♭sus2
B♭

C
B♭
Ah.
Ah.
Repeat ad lib.
Dm
Six o' clock on the au - - - - to - - - route.
Lights flash past like mem - - - - o - - - ries.
B♭
A

Dm
Burn - ing rub - ber, burn - ing chrome. Bay of Ca - diz and
speed - ing head, a speed - ing heart. I'm be - ing born, a
C
B♭add9
fer - ry home. At - lan - tic sea. Cut
bleed - ing start. The en - gines roar, blood
B♭
C
glass. Af - ri - can sun
curd - ling wail. Head first then
B♭add9
B♭
To Coda
at last.
foot then heart sets sail.

C
B♭
Ah.
Ah.
D
E
C
D.S. al Coda
Coda
D

E
C
G
8va
Bm
F♯m
A
A
A

WHITE AS SNOW

Music: Traditional, arranged by U2, Brian Eno & Daniel Lanois
Words by U2, Brian Eno & Daniel Lanois

Em Bm Am Bm Em
I came from there were no hills at all.
(3.) this dry ground, it bears no fruit at all.
Cmaj7 D Am
The land was flat, the high - way straight and
On - ly pop - pies laugh un - der a cresc - ent moon.
Em Am F C
wide. My broth - er and I would drive for hours, like we'd
The road re - fus - es stran - gers, the land,
G D Em Am
years in - stead of days. Our fac - es as pale as the
the seeds we sow. Where might we find a land as

D G
dir - ty snow.
white as snow?
4. As
Em Bm Am Bm Em
2. Once I knew there was a love div - ine,
boys we would go hunt - ing in the woods
Cmaj7 D Am
then came a time I thought it knew me not.
to sleep the night shoot - ing out the
Em Am
Who can for - give for -
stars.
Now the wolves are ev - 'ry

F C G D
give - ness, where for - give - ness is not? On -
pass - ing stran - ger, ev - 'ry face we can - not know. If on - ly a
Em Am D G
To Coda
-ly the land as white as snow.
heart could be as white as
D F Am Em
D F C Em
And the wa - ter, it was i - cy as it washed

C
Em
Am
C
o - ver me. And the moon shone a - bove,
Em
D
D.S. al Coda
'bove me.
3. Now
Coda
G
Em
Am
D
snow. If on - ly a heart could be as white as
G
snow.

BREATHE

Words by Bono
Music by U2

D5 A5 B5 A5
5fr 5fr 7fr 5fr
1. Six - teenth of June, nine - o - five, door - bell rings. Man at the door says if I
B5 A5 B5 D5 A5
7fr 5fr 7fr 5fr 5fr
wan - na stay a - live a bit long - er, there's three
B5 A5 B5 A5 B5
7fr 5fr 7fr 5fr 7fr
things I need you to know. Three.
D5 A5
5fr 5fr
2. Com - ing from a long line of tra - vel - ling sales__ peo - ple on my
3. Six - teenth of June, Chi - nese stocks are go - ing__ up and I'm

B5 A5 B5 A5 B5
7fr 5fr
moth-er's side, I was-n't gon-na buy just an-y-one's cock-a-
com-ing down with some new A-sian vi-rus.
D5 A5
-too. So why would I in-vite a com-plete stran-
Ju Ju man, Ju Ju man, Doc
-ger in-to my home? Would you? These
says you're fine or dy-ing. Please.
N.C.
days are bet-ter than that.
Nine-o-nine Saint John Di-vine on the line. My pulse is fine.
𝄋: Instrumental till *

These days are
But I'm run-ning down the road like loose e-lec-tric-i-ty while the
G
bet-ter than that.
band in my head plays a strip-tease.
Ev-
The
* We are peo-
D/F#
E
-ry day I die a-gain and a-gain I'm re-
roar that lies on the oth-er side of si-lence.
-ple borne of sound. The songs are in our eyes.

G D/F♯ E
born. Ev - 'ry day I have to find the cou-rage to…
The for - est fire that is fear so de - ny it.
Gon-na wear them like a crown, oh.
Bm Gsus2 D E
Walk out in - to the street with
Walk out in - to the street sing your
Walk out in-to a sun - burst street.
Bm Gsus2 D G6
arms out. Got a love you can't de - feat. Neith-er down
heart out. The peo - ple we meet will not be drowned
Sing your heart out. Sing my heart out.

Bm
Gsus2
D
E
nor out.
out.
There's noth - ing you have that I
I found grace in - side a sound.
𝄋 I found grace, it's all I found.
D5
A5
B5
A5
B5
A5
B5
need.
I can breathe.
𝄋 And I can breathe.
To Coda ⊕
D5
A5
B5
A5
B5
A5
B5
Breathe now.
Dsus4
D
E5
B♭5
B♭6
Csus4
C
Repeat ad lib.

N.C.
D.S. al Coda
Coda
Dsus4
D
E5
2fr
1, 3.
2.
B♭5
B♭6
Csus4
C
B♭5
B♭dim
Csus2
C
4.
B♭5
B♭dim
Csus2
C
D

CEDARS OF LEBANON

Words by Bono
Music by U2, Brian Eno, Daniel Lanois & Harold Budd

Oringinal key E♭ minor

Em
Bm/F♯
Em
1. Yes-ter-day I spent a-sleep.
Woke up in my clothes_ in a dir-ty
G/D
Em
Bm/F♯
heap.
Spent the night try-ing to make that dead-line.
Em
Squeez-ing com-pli-ca-ted lives in-to a sim-ple head-line.
Em
Bm/F♯
2. I have your face in an old po-la-roid,
3. Have-n't been with a wo-man, it feels like, for years.

Em
G/D
ti - dy - ing the child - ren's clothes and toys.
Thought of you the whole time, your salt - y tears.
Em
Bm/F♯
You're smil - ing back at me. I took the pho - to from the fridge.
This shit - ty world some - times pro - duc - es a rose.
Em
G/B
Can't re - mem - ner what then we did.
The scent of it lin - gers but then it just goes.
Em
G/D
Re - turn the call to

Cmaj7
Em
G/D
home.
Em/B
Bm/F♯
3
The worst_ of us are a long drawn out con-fes-sion.
Child drink-ing dir-ty wa-ter from the riv-er bank.
1° 𝄋 Instrumental
Now I've got a head like a litcig-a-rette.
Em
G/B
The best of us___ are ge - nius-es of___ com-pres-sion.
Sol-dier brings o-ran-ges he___ got out from a tank.
Un-ho - ly clouds re-flect in a min - ar-et.

Bm/F♯
You say you're not gon-na leave the truth a-lone.
I'm wait-ing on the wait-er, he's tak-ing a while to come.
You're so high a-bove me, high-er than ev-'ry-one.
1, 3, 4.
2.
Em
To Coda
G/B
I'm here 'cause I don't wan-na go home.
Watch-ing the sun go down on Le-ba-non.
Where are you in the Ce-dars of Le-ba-non.
Le-ba-non. Re-
Em
G/D
Cmaj7
Gmaj7
D.S. al Coda
-turn the call to home.
Coda
Gmaj7
N.C.
N.C.
8vb

N.C.
Choose your en - e - mies care - ful - ly 'cause the will de - fine you.
Make them in - t'res - ting 'cause in some ways they will mind you.
They're not there in the be - gin - ning but when your sto - ry ends.
Gon - na last with you long - er than your friends.

1 2 3 4 5 6 7 8 9